Junior Petkeeper's Library

GUINEA PIGS

Fiona Henrie

Consultant Editor
Michael Findlay M.R.C.V.S.

Photographs by Marc Henrie A.S.C.

Franklin Watts
London New York Sydney Toronto 1980

Franklin Watts Limited
8 Cork Street
London W1

© 1980 Franklin Watts Limited

SBN UK edition: 85166 857 7
SBN US edition: 531 04185 9
Library of Congress Catalog Card No: 80 50482

Printed in Great Britain by
Tindal Press, Chelmsford, Essex

The publisher and author would like to thank Christine Peachy for her
help in preparing this book.

Contents

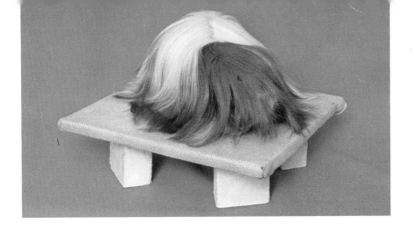

Proper food and care will help keep your guinea pig in good condition.

Introduction

Guinea pigs are live animals, not toys. They can feel hot or cold, hungry or satisfied. They can feel afraid or safe, comfortable or in pain.

Guinea pigs need to be looked after all the time. They usually live to be four or five years old. Guinea pigs kept in warm, dry climates may live to be seven years old.

A guinea pig costs money each week to feed and look after. You will need your parents' permission to keep a guinea pig, as you may need their help to care for it.

Guinea pigs are also called cavies. They are gentle creatures, interesting to care for and maybe to show.

Note to parents

If you decide to have a guinea pig in your household, please be sure that it is wanted by your child, yourself and your family, and that the interest will not wear off after the first few weeks.

You must be sure that you are willing to supervise its care and well being, and to cover the cost of its upkeep.

It would be unfair to the animal, to you, your child and your family to become unwilling pet owners.

Choosing a guinea pig

You may know a pet owner whose female guinea pig has had young. Schools which keep guinea pigs may have young for sale.

You can also buy guinea pigs from a breeder or a shop. If you buy your guinea pig from a shop, be quite sure that it is a clean place with a good reputation for healthy animals. When you buy a guinea pig at a shop, you may not know where it originally came from.

If you would like to breed pedigree guinea pigs, buy one from a breeder as you must know your pet's parentage.

6

Be sure that the guinea pig you choose is healthy. It should be able to walk and run easily. Its coat should be smooth and glossy, and the body firm and well rounded.

The guinea pig should have bright, clear eyes, and clean ears, nose and mouth. Its breathing should be quiet and even.

It is best to buy a guinea pig when it is between four and six weeks old. If you are able, buy two guinea pigs as they enjoy company. Unless you want to breed guinea pigs, choose two females as male guinea pigs will fight with each other.

A healthy guinea pig will be bright-eyed, and have soft, smooth fur and a firm body.

Preparing for your pet

Before you go to collect your guinea pig, you will need to buy a hutch. A wooden rabbit hutch will be suitable.

The hutch must be strong and dry, without any sharp parts inside which could hurt the animal. It must also be large enough for the guinea pig to have plenty of room to move around.

The hutch should be divided into a living area and a sleeping area. There should be a door of solid wood in front of the sleeping area, and a door covered with wire netting in front of the living area.

An outdoor hutch needs to be

If the weather is very cold and you have no outdoor shelter for your guinea pig, bring the hutch or pen indoors at night.

weather-proof. It is best to have a hutch with a sloping roof so that the rain runs off.

On cold nights cover the roof of the hutch with a piece of sacking, old carpet or roofing felt. You can also cover the back and the sides of the hutch with roofing felt for extra warmth.

Guinea pigs are most comfortable in temperatures of 16–20 °C (60–68 °F). The best position for an outside hutch is facing south-east.

In winter put the hutch in a shed which is dry and well ventilated. Do not keep the hutch in a garage as car fumes are poisonous.

Attach the water bottle to the bars of the hutch and see that it is low enough for the guinea pig to reach the spout, but not so low that the spout touches the floor. Refill the bottle every day or whenever it is empty.

If you keep one or two guinea pigs, you will need a hutch approximately 90 × 45 × 30 cm (36 × 18 × 12 in) in size. Put an outdoor hutch on a shelf or frame 60 cm (24 in) high.

Varnish the floor of the hutch to stop the wood rotting. Put varnish on the inside of the hutch, too, or line it with linoleum. This makes the hutch easier to clean. Check that the varnish is safe for animals. Do not use paint as it is poisonous for guinea pigs. Put a layer of litter and some bedding on the hutch floor.

Your guinea pig will also need a food dish and a water bottle. Buy enough food for the first few days.

10

Taking your pet home

When you collect your guinea pig, make sure that you have a strong container, such as a large, dry cardboard box in which to carry it home.

Punch some holes near the top of the box for ventilation. Put some fresh hay on the bottom of the box to make the guinea pig comfortable, and give it a little food.

Find out from the previous owner the sex and age of the guinea pig, and which foods it is used to eating. Return home as quickly as you can so that the guinea pig will not be too upset by the journey.

Above left
When you take your guinea pig home, see that the box is well ventilated. A few holes punched near the top of the box will be sufficient.

Above right
A little hay at the bottom of the carrying box will make the guinea pig feel more comfortable.

11

Food

Give your guinea pig some green food each day. Each day remove old, uneaten green food and give the guinea pig a fresh supply. Wash the food dish every day with hot water before filling it with fresh food.

Guinea pigs must have vitamin C. They get this from green plants—the main part of their diet—fruit and some root vegetables.

Guinea pigs are bulk feeders, which means they like to eat throughout the day, so see that there is food in the hutch at all times. Put fresh food into the dish in the morning and in the evening, or just in the evening.

Guinea pigs need clean, fresh water to drink at all times.

A bowl of water in the hutch gets dirty quickly. A gravity-flow water bottle attached to the side of the hutch will keep the water clean.

12

Guinea pigs need to have some "wet" and some "dry" food each day. Wet foods are fruit and vegetables. Dry foods are cereal and grain, either fed dry or wet in a mash. Make a mash from cereal, grain, small pieces of wholewheat bread, potato peelings or cooked potatoes mixed with a little water.

In summer you can give your guinea pig green plants, such as dandelion and chickweed. As some plants are poisonous, only give your pet those plants which you know are safe. In winter, when green plants may be scarce, give your guinea pig root vegetables and extra mash.

These are some of the different foods you can give your guinea pig. The dark-blue bowl contains rabbit mix, and the other bowls contain grain and seed.

13

See that your guinea pig has plenty of fresh hay. Guinea pigs like to nibble hay as well as using it for bedding.

You can give your guinea pig rabbit or hamster food mix instead of fresh dry food.

The appetites of guinea pigs vary. You will soon learn how much your guinea pig eats each day. If the dish is empty, give larger meals. If there is much uneaten food, cut the portions down. Wash the food dish every day in hot water.

Give the guinea pig some fresh hay every day. You can also give it freshly-cut grass clippings, but check first that the grass has not been treated with chemicals.

14

Hygiene

Most guinea pigs use one corner of their hutch as their toilet. Put layers of newspaper on the bottom of the hutch. Cover the paper with about 5 cm (2 in) of sawdust, peat or cat litter. The litter will soak up the guinea pig's urine. Guinea pig droppings look like small roundish, brown pellets. They will be firm if the animal is healthy.

Take out the droppings and the damp litter each day. If the hutch is kept clean, there will be no bad smells. A hutch with one guinea pig in it needs to be cleaned thoroughly each week.

Spread an even layer of litter—about 5 cm (2 in) thick—on the bottom of the hutch. Remove wet and dirty litter from the cage every day.

Before you begin to clean the hutch, take out the guinea pig and put it somewhere safe. Put it in a cardboard box, or a spare hutch or cage if you have one. Put some fresh hay and a little food in the bottom of the container.

Take out all the old food and the food bowl, and unclip the water bottle. Remove all the old bedding and litter, and the newspaper from the floor of the hutch. Wrap up everything in a large piece of newspaper and throw it away.

Use a paint scraper or a piece of old cutlery to clean out the difficult corners. Afterwards brush out the loose pieces.

16

Wash the inside of the hutch with hot, soapy water and disinfectant. Make sure the disinfectant is one which is safe for animals. Dry the hutch thoroughly before putting the guinea pig back. A guinea pig may catch a cold, bronchitis or even pneumonia in a damp hutch.

Put clean newspaper, litter and bedding in the hutch. Refill the water bottle and clip it on to the side of the hutch. Put fresh food into the dish and some green food into the hutch.

Wash your hands after cleaning your guinea pig's hutch and whenever you handle the guinea pig—especially before eating.

When you have dried the hutch and replaced all the things your pet needs—clean litter and bedding, fresh food and water— you can put the guinea pig back into its home.

You can buy litter in large plastic sacks which last a long time.

Activity

Guinea pigs are diurnal creatures. This means that they sleep at night and are active during the day. Guinea pigs may not seem very lively in the hutch, but if you let them out in a room or a garden, you will see how quickly they move.

If you have a garden, let your guinea pig exercise on the lawn during warm weather. Make sure that the grass has not been treated with any chemicals.

Put the guinea pig in a special outdoor run—a large frame covered with wire netting. Make a shelter at one end of the run.

18

Handling

Guinea pigs are quite timid, nervous creatures, although they hardly ever bite. Gradually handle your pet more and more each day, so that it becomes used to you.

Pick up a guinea pig like this. Slide one hand under the guinea pig's body, and then place the other hand on top of the guinea pig to steady it and lift it up. Always support the guinea pig's weight firmly.

Never pick up a guinea pig by the scruff of its neck or its stomach, or hold it near the front of its body.

When you hold a guinea pig in the palm of one hand, use the other hand to support and steady the animal.

The correct way to pick up a guinea pig. Put one hand beneath the guinea pig's body and use the other hand to support the animal as you lift it up.

19

Breeding

Do not breed guinea pigs unless you are sure you can provide good homes for the young. The ideal age for a first mating is five months.

You will need a mature boar (male) and one or two mature sows (females)— all in perfect health.

If you are going to keep the young, you will need three extra hutches. One hutch is for the boar after the sow is "in pig" (pregnant). The second hutch is for the young when they leave the sow,

20

and the third hutch is for when the males are separated from the females.

Female guinea pig with one of her litter. Separate the young from the mother after they have been weaned.

When you know that the sow is in pig, put the boar into his own hutch, or he could mate the sow again as soon as the litter is born.

A few days before the litter is due, clean the cage very carefully. Although guinea pigs do not build nests, they will need extra hay for bedding.

Young are born about ten weeks after a successful mating. Guinea pigs usually have two or three young.

21

The vet in this picture is examining a female guinea pig and her litter. Contact your vet whenever you are worried about your guinea pig's health.

Determining the sex of a guinea pig.

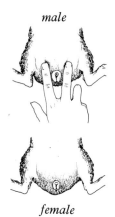

male

female

Gently press each side of the guinea pig's sex organs. With the male the pressure will cause the penis to protrude slightly.

When the litter arrives, do not disturb the sow or the young for twenty-four hours.

Guinea pigs are born with hair. Their eyes are open, and they are able to move about. After two or three days the young are able to eat a little solid food. They will suckle milk from the sow for about three weeks.

If you are going to keep the young, you will need extra hutches. When the young are fully weaned (eating solid food), remove them from the mother. Separate the males from the females within five weeks as they are able to mate at that age.

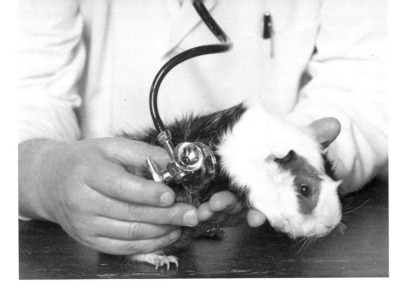

Health

If you are worried about your guinea pig's health, contact your vet. Do not try to treat your pet yourself.

Signs of illness in your pet are:
- if it lies or crouches in the hutch without moving;
- if it refuses to eat its food;
- if its fur is dull, spiky, or falling out;
- if it is having difficulty in breathing, or if its breathing is loud or uneven;
- if it has diarrhea or constipation;
- if it is dragging its hind legs or is finding it difficult to move about;
- if it is coughing or sneezing, or has a runny nose or eyes.

23

Grooming a long-haired guinea pig.

Grooming and care

A short-haired guinea pig has a smooth, even coat with a sheen on it. Use a small, soft brush or a piece of pure silk to keep the shine. Brush or stroke the guinea pig from head to tail.

Groom the Abyssinian, or rough-haired, guinea pig with a toothbrush. Brush from the middle of each whorl (or rosette) outwards.

Groom a long-haired guinea pig like this. Brush and comb the hair downwards from the middle of the guinea pig's back. Unless you want to show a long-haired guinea pig, you

24

may find it more practical to cut its hair short.

Guinea pigs have long front teeth, called incisors, which grow all the time. If they grow too long, the guinea pig may have difficulty eating.

A vet can cut the teeth to the right length. Never try to cut the teeth yourself. If you give the guinea pig a block of hard wood to gnaw on, it will help to wear the teeth down.

The nails can also grow too long. Your vet can clip them. He may show your parents or you how to do this in the future.

Long-haired show guinea pigs have their hair put in curlers (made of stiff paper) to keep it from becoming tangled.

There will be time for a final grooming before the guinea pig is judged.

Take your guinea pig to the show in a special carrying box. You can buy carrying boxes in different sizes. Some are for one animal only, while others hold two, three or four.

Shows

Various clubs and associations hold specialist shows for guinea pigs. Sometimes agricultural or livestock shows have a section where guinea pigs can be exhibited. There may be sections for both pure-bred guinea pigs and for pet guinea pigs.

A guinea pig must be in perfect health and top condition before entering a show. When you decide to show your guinea pig, prepare it a few weeks beforehand with daily grooming.

Take your guinea pig to the show in

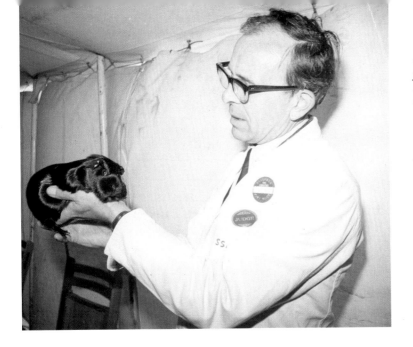

Guinea pig being judged at a show. Pet guinea pigs are judged on their health and ease of handling. Pure-bred guinea pigs are judged on their shape, eyes, shade and markings. These standards vary according to the different breeds.

Guinea pigs in show pens. Give your guinea pig some food and water while it is in the pen.

a strong, clean, well-ventilated carrying box. Put sawdust, hay and a piece of green food in the box for the journey.

At small shows guinea pigs stay in their carrying boxes until it is time for them to be judged. At large shows guinea pigs are put into show cages. Each cage has a number on it for identification. A steward collects each guinea pig and takes it to the judging table. The guinea pig must sit still while it is being judged. Afterwards the steward returns it to its cage.

A steward takes each guinea pig to the judge, and returns the animal to its pen after it has been examined.

27

Tortoiseshell guinea pig photographed from behind to show the markings.

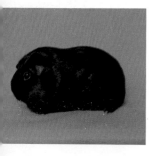

Chocolate self guinea pig. Selfs are the same shade all over their bodies.

About guinea pigs

Guinea pigs or cavies are rodents. Rodents are animals with long front teeth, which are used for gnawing.

Guinea pigs originally come from South America. "Cavy" is the name given to these animals by the Peruvian Indians. No one is sure where the name "guinea pig" comes from. It may have been the name used by sailors from Guiana (now Guyana). Guinea pigs are not related to pigs in any way, although the males are called boars and the females are called sows.

28

Abyssinian dark brindle—a rough-haired guinea pig.

Abyssinian blue roan—a rough-haired guinea pig.

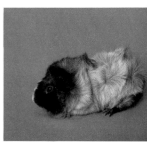

A Peruvian slate and orange—a long-haired guinea pig.

Varieties of guinea pigs

There are three types of guinea pig coats—short-haired (smooth), rough-haired and long-haired.

The short-haired types are known as English, American or Bolivian guinea pigs. One short-haired guinea pig, the American Crested, has a smooth coat and a crest of long hair on its head.

The Abyssinian guinea pig is rough-haired, with a short, coarse coat which grows in whorls. The Peruvian guinea pig is long-haired. It has very long, silky hair covering its body and face.

29

Checklist

Before you get your guinea pig you will need
- a hutch or cage
- a food dish and a gravity-flow water bottle
- sawdust, wood shavings, peat or cat litter
- bedding
- food for the first few days
- a container to carry the guinea pig home
- a gnawing block

Each day
- Change the water
- Feed the guinea pig once or twice a day
- Remove the wet and dirty litter from the hutch
- Check that the pet is active and healthy
- Groom a long-haired guinea pig

Each week
- Clean the cage or hutch completely
- Check your supplies of food, litter and bedding

When necessary
- Prepare the guinea pig for a show
- Buy or make extra hutches for young guinea pigs
- If your guinea pig is sick, take it to the vet and follow the vet's instructions carefully.

Glossary

Boar   male guinea pig.

Bulk feeder   animal which needs to eat regularly throughout the day.

Diurnal animal   animal which is active during the day and sleeps at night.

Grooming   taking care of the coat by brushing and combing.

In pig   pregnant guinea pig.

Litter   absorbent material put in the bottom of the hutch to soak up urine.

Litter   more than one young born to one mother at the same time.

Mash   cereal, grain, wholemeal bread, small pieces of cooked potatoes or potato peelings added to a little water to make a crumbly mixture.

Scruff   loose skin at the back of the guinea pig's neck.

Sow   female guinea pig.

Weaning   getting the young used to eating solid food instead of suckling their mother's milk.

Index